Gus the Gulping G

Gus the **g**oat loved to **g**ulp yo**g**hurt, **G**us couldn't **g**et enough – he could **g**ulp **g**allons of it all at once!

-g-g-g-g-g-g-g-g-g-g-g-g-g-g-g-g-

Gus kept yoghurt in his wagon so he could drag it everywhere he went. Whenever he wanted a gulp, his jug of yoghurt was right there.

Along **g**alloped Ma**gg**ie the **g**oat.
She liked to **g**ulp yo**g**hurt too.

She **g**ulped a ju**g** of yo**g**hurt in
the morning, noon and night.

She **g**ulped yo**g**hurt in the **g**arden.

Maggie gulped yoghurt in the garage.

She **g**ulped yo**g**hurt by Dou**g** the pi**g** in the pig pen.

"You've **g**ot yo**g**hurt!? I love yo**g**hurt. In fact,
I am the best at **g**ulping yo**g**hurt," said Ma**gg**ie.

"No you're not! I am the best,
and the fastest," <u>**G**</u>us declared.

"Well let's **g**ulp this yo**g**hurt to**g**ether, and see who wins!" **G**us said.

So they each grabbed a ju**g** and started to **g**ulp the yo**g**hurt.

-g-g-g-g-g-g-g-g-g-g-g-g-

Gulp **g**ulp **g**ulp! Faster and faster!

Lots of animals **g**athered around to see who would win the **g**ulping race. Dou**g** Pi**g** and Tee**g**an Ti**g**er sat **g**iggling to**g**ether with glee.

Gus **g**ulped more yo**g**hurt and faster than
he ever had **g**ulped before. With one last big **g**ulp,
Gus finished his yo**g**hurt…. First! All the animals
gathered around cheered.

Just then **G**us let loose a bi**g** hiccup which made everyone **gigg**le. Hiccup hiccup! **G**us couldn't stop! The animals laughed even harder at poor **G**us.

Now **G**us **g**ets the hiccups every time he **g**ulps his yo**g**hurt – and all the animals call him '**G**us the **g**ulping **g**oat'…

... But it never gets in his way!